THE
BIRD
BOOK

A CURIOUS COMPENDIUM OF
50 WILD BIRDS

Written by Dr Meriel Lland and Roxy Furman
Illustrated by Nicola Howell Hawley

A STUDIO PRESS BOOK

First published in the UK in 2021 by Studio Press,
an imprint of Bonnier Books UK,
The Plaza, 535 King's Road,
London SW10 0SZ
Owned by Bonnier Books,
Sveavägen 56, Stockholm, Sweden

www.studiopressbooks.co.uk
www.bonnierbooks.co.uk

Text © Studio Press Books 2021
Illustrations © Nicola Howell Hawley 2021

www.howellillustration.co.uk

1 3 5 7 9 10 8 6 4 2

ISBN 978-1-78741-974-2

Written by Dr Meriel Lland and Roxy Furman
Illustrated by Nicola Howell Hawley
Edited by Sophie Blackman
Designed by Rob Ward
Production by Emma Kidd

A CIP catalogue for this book is available from the British Library.

Printed and bound in China

CONTENTS

HOW TO SPOT BIRDS

THE WILD BEYOND YOUR WINDOW

This book is an invitation to explore. Welcome to the wild world of birds and birding. Look out of your window, or step out of your door, look up into the skies and you will discover a whole universe of twittering, fluttering, soaring, swooping life.

Birds breathe alongside us in cities, towns and villages and their journeys are intricately interwoven with our own. But each bird has its own story. Come

to know the secret lives of birds and you will develop a deeper understanding of the world around us. You will witness new dramas in every month of the year: stories of epic flights of endurance, incomparable resilience, unbreakable pair-bonds, devoted parenting and struggles for life. As the chill of winter gives way to spring, new generations will take to the air. Familiar yet mysterious, we have so much to learn about these wild beauties.

How to use this book

This book is more a series of character sketches than a comprehensive field guide. It is an introduction to 50 of our most recognisable birds. Alongside a depiction of the male (as they tend to have the more distinctive plumage), and notes on variations between the sexes, you'll find an overview of each species, what makes it distinctive, a map of where you might find it and what it's like to see and hear the bird in its habitat.

Take this book with you when you're out and about on walks, cycles or on bigger adventures, such as camping and paragliding! You'll discover the essence of each bird – its plumage, voice and habits. Look beneath their metaphorical feathers and you'll discover something of the birds' folk history and place in culture. Hopefully you'll be hooked, so there are resources on page 112 that will help you take your interest further.

The gift of noticing

Birding is about noticing. To spot birds, you don't need expensive equipment – just use your eyes and ears. Inexpensive binoculars will help but they are not essential. The key to identifying birds – or 'making an ID' as birders say – is thinking about how you encounter them. Notice the season, the habitat and their behaviour. Use the illustrations here as a starting point. Keep a note of what you see and where you see it. But most of all, take time to look and listen.

Explore your local wild patch and visit often. Science has taught us that time in nature is healing, and birding can be mindfulness in action. Birds can connect us with the wider world and shift our perspective, helping us see beyond our personal situation. Spot an unexpected species or learn something new about a species you already know, and it never fails to feel like a gift. Enjoy!

HABITATS
TOP TIPS FOR FINDING BIRDS

This book is divided into colour-coded habitats but, remember, birds don't read field guides and frequently visit more than one environment! This book will help you get a sense of where to look to increase the number of birds you spot.

Gardens

Green spaces around our homes connect us with the wild. From the window, balcony or garden, watch and learn who visits your patch and when. Our homes make superb bird hides. Provide water, food and shelter and the birds will come. Watch out for neighbourhood cats and situate any feeders well out of reach of predators.

Parks and urban oases

Parks bring people and birds together. Areas with mature trees, shrubs and grassland are especially rich. Berried trees are particularly popular, while lawns attract species looking for worms and insects. Lakes and ponds are a magnet for waterbirds.

Towns and cities

Street pigeons are only the beginning! Cityscapes are pulsing with birdlife, and our buildings, tree-lined streets and balconies offer extra sources of food and warmth. Rooftops and ledges are key places to spot birds. Some species use tall buildings to roost and breed as they would cliff faces. City rivers and canals also attract many species to water.

Freshwater

On weekend adventures by rivers, lakes or in wetlands, keep an eye on waterside banks, overhanging trees and mid-stream rocks where birds can often be found.

Agricultural land

A run or cycle along a quiet country lane is great for birding in every season. The richest locations are those on land that has been managed in traditional ways, with hedgerows (a haven for nesting species), small fields and mixed crops. As you walk, look for birds among livestock and follow tractor activity, as birds often hunt for food in ploughed soil.

Coasts

Where land meets the sea there are sandy beaches, rock pools, mudflats, cliffs, shingle, estuaries and dunes, all of which can attract birds. Look for waders on the shore as the tide recedes or take a boat ride to experience the sights and smells of a seabird colony.

Woodlands

As you hike along the tracks, look up into the canopy and down into the leaf-litter, paying particular attention to clearings and woodland edges, to spot something special.

Moorlands and Mountains

The remote locations we escape to when we need to de-stress and refresh are often the wildest places. As you hike or cycle along trails, listen for birdsong and look for movement against the skyline or on high points, such as fence posts. Birds often congregate near pools as water can be scarce in these environments.

HOW TO HELP LOCAL BIRDS
AND WHY WE NEED TO

The wild has always been essential to our lives. Open a window, step out of your door, look up into the sky and celebrate the birds you see there. Wildlife knows no national boundaries, and birds bring the wonder of the wider world up close. The help we can offer to the birds on our doorstep supports populations both at home and far away.

But the numbers of many species have declined in recent years. The IUCN (International Union for Conservation of Nature™) Red List is an international database that gives each species a conservation status, from Least Concern to Extinct. This book lists the IUCN status of each bird, as well as giving local conservation information.

In the UK, birds on the Red List are in severe decline. Amber is the next most critical group, and Green the least critical. Picking up this book is a great first step towards helping birds survive and thrive. Fortunately, there are many more things we can do to help, and here are a few suggestions.

When humans build on wild areas, and introduce certain agricultural practices, it reduces the space available for birds to nest and forage for food. If you have a garden, or even a window-box, a good way of creating a haven for local birds is to grow plants that are native to your area. This will provide natural shelter and will attract the bugs that birds like to eat. Even better: avoid pesticides in your

garden to help emulate natural habitats and preserve the ecosystem.

If you have the space, build a bird feeding station. Birds' favourite foods include sunflower seeds, unsalted peanuts, suet balls and, in the autumn, soft fruits like apples and pears. This will give birds a reliable source of food all year round, and a better chance of survival when natural shortages occur.

Birds need water daily, both to drink and to bathe in. Cold winters can be fatal for them as rivers and lakes freeze over. In hot summers, birds can overheat, and competition for resources can be fierce when migratory species arrive early with the warm weather. Leaving out a shallow dish of water all year round, changing it two to three times a week, can help ease seasonal challenges.

Another way of helping birds is to be mindful of what we consume and how we live. Making sure that our food – particularly fish – is sourced sustainably, reducing waste and limiting light pollution will all have an impact. We can each play our part in protecting the world we share with birds. Conservation organisations (see page 112) explain how we can help the planet and birds in more detail, including how to install nest-boxes – out of reach of local cats – and how to maintain feeders.

Once your garden or local area is thriving, you can join in with citizen science initiatives to count the birds that visit. As we deepen our understanding of the natural world, as the community of bird-lovers grows, and as we do what we can to help the birds in our local patch, there is hope that we can protect the dawn chorus for generations to come.

BLUE TIT
CYANISTES CAERULEUS

Out of the corner of your eye, if you spot a flash of blue, yellow, white and green, it is likely to be a blue tit. Seeing these little birds zipping back and forth with beaks full of moss is a sure sign that spring is upon us.

To their nests they add hair, leaves, feathers and even spiders' webs! They mainly choose holes in trees but are just as happy to use bird boxes. Blue tits usually raise a single brood each year. Eggs hatch in May, and chicks emerge for the world to see about three weeks later.

Blue tits are said to be the most attractive garden bird, but they are more than just a pretty face. They perform jaw-dropping acrobatic displays while on the hunt for their food, including their favourite: juicy caterpillars. It is these caterpillars that make their feathers a striking colour. They contain high levels of a pigment, known as carotene, which produces the bright yellow colour on the blue tits' chests.

These birds are not particularly fussy eaters, and will tuck into fruit, seeds and peanuts left out on bird feeders. Those who have their morning milk delivered to their doorstep may observe clever blue tits breaking through the foil bottle tops, drinking the creamy top layer inside!

In winter, blue tits join up with other tit species to visit gardens in large groups in search of food. When they are all together it can be a little challenging to tell them apart from great tits but look out for their defining bright blue caps – great tits' caps are black – and their smaller size.

'tsee-tsee-tsee'

Length:
12 cm

Wingspan:
18 cm

■ **IUCN status:** Least Concern
■ **UK status:** Green
■ **Visible:** All year

■ **Sexes:** Alike
■ **Voice:** High-pitched 'sispi si-hi-hi' call.
trilling 'tsee-tsee-tsee' song.

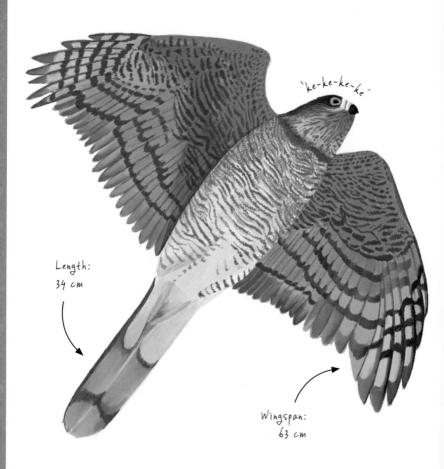

'ke-ke-ke-ke'

Length:
34 cm

Wingspan:
63 cm

- **IUCN status:** Least Concern
- **UK status:** Green
- **Visible:** All year

- **Sexes:** Differ, see opposite
- **Voice:** Shrieking 'ke-ke-ke-ke' call.

SPARROWHAWK
ACCIPITER NISUS

As you sit in your garden, watching birds dart to and from your feeder, a sparrowhawk appears from behind a hedgerow as if out of nowhere and seizes its prey: taking the bird (and you) by surprise! These small birds of prey rely on ambush and stealth, and gardens are an ideal hunting ground. Their diet is predominantly songbirds – thrushes, starlings, finches – although they will occasionally feast on small mammals.

As with most birds of prey, the female is larger – by up to twenty-five percent, which is one of the greatest size differences between sexes of any bird species. Their colouration is remarkably different too. Females have grey-brown upper parts compared to the males' bluish-grey appearance. Both sexes have much paler underparts. This 'countershading' breaks up the birds' outline against the sky in flight, so their prey is less likely to see them approach with their flap-flap-glide flight pattern. A perfectly crafted predator.

Sparrowhawk populations crashed during the agricultural boom that followed World War Two as more pesticides were used in farming. Once harmful chemicals were banned, populations recovered, and sparrowhawks are now one of the most common bird of prey species in Europe.

Once at home on the edge of woodlands, sparrowhawks are now just as likely to be spotted in the suburbs as they are in the countryside. You can see sparrowhawks at any time of the year, but the most exciting time to spot one is early spring, when males perform a territorial 'rollercoaster' flight, climbing high into the sky before diving back down again at stomach-churning speeds to ward off rivals and attract a mate.

CHAFFINCH
FRINGILLA COELEBS

The chaffinch is a frequent visitor to bird feeders all year round, preferring to pick up fallen seeds from the ground rather than feeding from the table itself. As the year progresses, these birds shift from a diet of insects in spring, to one of mainly seeds, and they forage both in trees and on the ground.

Listen out for their vast repertoire of powerful calls. Their song differs depending on their location – chaffinches are one of the few birds with regional accents! Their main call is a short, repetitive trill known as a 'rain call' in the UK, as it was believed to predict storms.

Chaffinches have had a difficult history with humans. Their beautiful song attracted attention, and wild chaffinches were caught and sold as caged songbirds. People would bet on the number of times each chaffinch would repeat its song. Though largely outlawed, the practice still continues with captive-bred birds in parts of Europe.

The male chaffinch is vibrantly coloured and unmistakable. He has a blue-grey cap, with pink or rust-red cheeks and underparts and white bars on his wings. Females are much duller in colour, covered in pale brown feathers with white bars on the wings and, occasionally, a green or yellowish tone to the rump.

They are abundant in the wild, with a breeding range extending across most of Europe. Breeding occurs from April to June, during which time the female will build a deep, cup nest within the fork of a tree and lay up to five eggs. Both the eggs and nestlings can become prey to crows, squirrels and domestic cats. If you have a garden, planting native trees and shrubs will ensure that these birds have places to hide their nests.

'chip chip chip chooee chooee chooee'

- **IUCN status:** Least Concern
- **UK status:** Green
- **Length:** 14.5 cm
- **Wingspan:** 27 cm
- **Visible:** All year

- **Sexes:** Differ, see opposite
- **Voice:** Song is 'chip chip chip chooe chooee chooee'. Call is a soft, whistled 'huuit'.

Listen for their trembling song ending with a 'trill....'

'teck-teck-teck'

- **IUCN status:** Least Concern
- **UK status:** Green
- **Length:** 9 cm
- **Wingspan:** 15 cm
- **Visible:** All year
- **Sexes:** Alike
- **Voice:** Alarm call is 'teck-teck-teck'.

WREN
TROGLODYTES TROGLODYTES

According to European folklore, the small but mighty wren is 'king of the birds'. In a fable about a flying competition between the wren and the eagle, the wren uses its intelligence to hitch a ride on the back of the eagle until the eagle has flown as high as it can. The wren then launches itself from the back of the eagle, winning the competition by flying highest and becoming 'king'.

Many local names for the wren across Europe include the word 'king'. In France, *roitelet* means 'little king', while the Dutch name, *winterkoninkje*, means 'winter-king'. The wren may not be a natural high-flier, but it has a truly regal voice, and you can witness its power and strength as it sings all year round.

These plump, brown birds have short necks and a tail that they often hold vertically. They are one of Europe's most common breeding birds and are regular garden visitors. Wrens are busy birds and are constantly searching for food. Moving with quick jerks, their tiny, rounded wings almost whir to keep them airborne for short, low-level flights before they probe their pin-sharp beaks into crevices. Insects form the bulk of their diet, mainly the larvae of moths and butterflies, as well as spiders – so this bird should be popular with arachnophobes!

The male builds several nests to attract females and, unlike most songbirds, will breed with three to four females in his territory at once. He will display to any potential mate; posturing and singing, with his wings and tail half open. Sometimes he will extend one wing, then raise and lower it several times in quick succession. The female will then choose her favourite nest, lining it generously with feathers in preparation for her chicks.

SONG THRUSH
TURDUS PHILOMELOS

Leaving home on an early spring morning, you may be greeted by the melodic tones of a male song thrush singing from the treetops. His song is hugely varied and includes more than one hundred phrases. This distinctive voice has been honoured by nature poets in England, including William Wordsworth and Thomas Hardy.

In France, these birds are known as the 'musical thrush'. They are also remarkable mimics, not just of birdsong, but of sounds like a ringing telephone.

The song thrush is brown, with a cream tummy speckled with black, and warm-yellow underwings – or sides. It can be confused with the mistle thrush, but the song thrush is smaller, browner and has different shaped speckles. These birds can also occasionally be mistaken for redwings, but the song thrush lacks the redwing's white eye stripe and orange-red underwings.

Like blackbirds, they hunt by sight. You can watch them run, stop, then run again across open ground before rummaging through leaf-litter to pick out earthworms.

Thrushes vary their diet by feasting on snails. These clever birds use stones as tools, smashing the snails into them, like an anvil, to crack the shell and extract the tasty body within.

The breeding season starts early for these birds all across Europe. Females typically lay three broods of up to six glossy, blue eggs. Their cup-shaped nests are built low down in the trees and are held together with smooth mud and saliva. After the eggs hatch, both parents help to feed the young, darting to and from the nest with food.

- **IUCN status:** Least Concern
- **UK status:** Red
- **Length:** 23 cm
- **Wingspan:** 34 cm
- **Visible:** All year
- **Sexes:** Alike
- **Voice:** Complex song including short, sharp 'tsip' call.

Recognisable from their elaborate, musical song:

'filip filip filip codidio codidio codidio,

quit quit quit, tittit tittit

tittit, tereret tereert tereert...'

repeated two to four times.

- **IUCN status:** Least Concern
- **UK status:** Green
- **Length:** 14 cm
- **Wingspan:** 21 cm

- **Visible:** All year
- **Sexes:** Alike
- **Voice:** They give a warbling 'twiddle-oo' song. Alarm call is a loud 'tic'.

'twiddle-oo'

'twiddle-oo'

ROBIN
ERITHACUS RUBECULA

On a frosty winter morning, as you head outside to take in the crisp weather, you are likey to be joined by nature's Christmas star: the robin redbreast. Although associated with the festive season, these charismatic little birds are resident in much of Europe all year round, and their distinctive, bright, orangey-red breasts have brought them fame.

Despite their charming appearance, robins are aggressive and attack competitors that stray into their territory. Disputes between males are often fatal, accounting for up to ten percent of adult robin deaths.

Some robins learn to trust people. If a little visitor swoops in to pick out some earthworms from your freshly turned garden soil, it is likely to be a robin. Folklore recognised robins as gardeners' friends and warned that if any robins were killed or injured, bad luck would result. Irish folk traditions went so far as to say that the killing of a robin would lead to a permanent tremor in the hand that struck the blow! It is not only humans that robins approach, but large animals like wild boar, who disturb the soil as they search for food, bringing insects to the surface. During the winter, robins supplement their invertebrate diet with berries, fruit and seed mixtures from bird tables.

The robins' lack of fear sometimes extends to choosing a breeding site; they will nest in anything from natural crevices to barbecues, bicycle handlebars, watering cans and flowerpots. Their cylindrical-shaped nests are made of moss, grass, hair and lined with feathers. Robins lay a couple of egg clutches during spring. When the fledglings emerge a few weeks later, look out for mottled brown babies hopping around, learning what it takes to become a seasonal celebrity!

GREEN WOODPECKER

PICUS VIRIDIS

As you take a shortcut through the park, the bruise-grey sky threatening a storm, you may hear a loud, eerie cackle. Looking in the direction of the laughter, you see a vivid-green bird take to the air. This is the 'yaffle', or green woodpecker. Yaffle is one of the old British country names for this bird, and it represents its yelping call.

Unlikely as it seems, yaffles are well camouflaged. Their soft, green plumage is tricky to spot when they are searching for ants, their favourite food, on the grass. It is in flight that the woodpecker's vibrant feathers can be seen. The lemony-yellow rump, green back and red head make it look more like a rainforest bird than resident of a town park.

Green woodpeckers select breeding sites close to the woodland edge. They prefer softwood trees that are easy for them to excavate, and they will often repurpose old nest holes to avoid drilling new ones. Their beaks aren't made for the powered carpentry of the stronger great spotted woodpeckers. The established trees and wide expanses of grassland make town parks an almost perfect habitat for them.

The courtship ritual for this species is an intense game of hide and seek around a tree trunk, with both the male and the female sporting raised, red crown feathers and fanned wings. The sexes are very similar, but the male has a thin, red moustache. These are difficult to see as yaffles are shy and not easy to approach. Young birds have more muted versions of the adult plumage.

As you continue through the park and the promised rain begins to fall, remember that another old British country name for the yaffle was 'rain bird', as its haunting call was said to foretell storms to come.

'kee-ooo, kee-ooo, kee-ooo'

'kee-ooo, kee-ooo'

- **IUCN status:** Least Concern
- **UK status:** Green
- **Length:** 34 cm
- **Wingspan:** 49 cm
- **Visible:** All year
- **Sexes:** Differ, see opposite
- **Voice:** Call is a noisy 'kee-ooo, kee-ooo'.

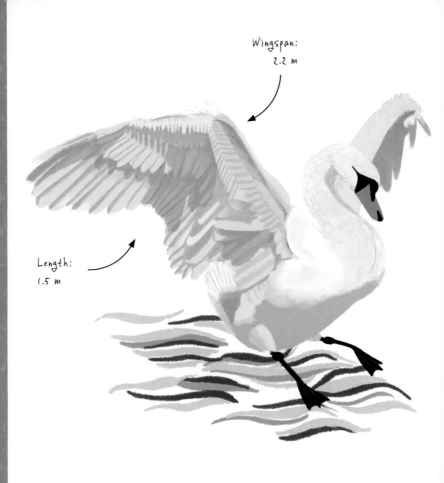

Wingspan: 2.2 m

Length: 1.5 m

- **IUCN status:** Least Concern
- **UK status:** Amber
- **Visible:** All year
- **Sexes:** Alike
- **Voice:** Hissing when angry and snorting 'heeehorr'.

MUTE SWAN
CYGNUS OLOR

On an autumn morning, as sunlight breaks through the mist and the lake sparkles, there's a rhythmic whining overhead as wingbeats cut the air. A pair of swans glide down onto the water, perfect companions serenely slipping into the mist.

Mute swans, one of Europe's largest breeding birds, are instantly recognisable and much misunderstood. They can't break a human leg with a single blow of a wing, not all British swans are owned by the Queen and they are not mute!

Swans make many noises. They growl, snort, cough and the females make a quack-like sound when calling to their silver-grey, downy cygnets. Be wary of the swan's hiss. These birds are fearless defenders of their young. Anyone wandering too close to a nest will be confronted with a hissing display and raised feathers. This is enough to deter most enemies but if the intruder doesn't retreat then the swan will attack, hitting out with the front edge of their powerful, bony wings and biting with a large, serrated beak. These are loyal birds that will protect their family to the death.

In winter, other swan species may appear from the far north, but they are usually less approachable than the mute swan. The visitors' beaks are bright yellow and black, while mute swans' beaks are vivid orange. The male, or cob, can be identified in spring by the large, black bulge that grows on top of his beak. This lessens after the breeding season. The female, a pen, has a more elegant beak, but for most of the year the sexes are difficult to tell apart.

One of the widespread rumours about mute swans is true, though: they are faithful birds that usually mate for life.

GREAT CRESTED GREBE
PODICEPS CRISTATUS

As the late spring sun begins to rise, casting long shadows onto the lake, two slender birds call across the water. They glide towards each other, bobbing their heads in mirroring motions. These are great crested grebes, and this display is the overture to one of the most intricate ritual courtships in the bird kingdom. In unison, they raise the elaborate head crests that gave them their name, and the 'weed' or 'penguin' dance begins.

Each grebe dives down into the water to collect a posy of waterweeds. With crests erect, they swim away. They then turn around and each swims back towards the other at top speed with their heads low. At the last minute they paddle to raise themselves out of the water. Then, almost standing, they look more penguin-like than grebe-like. This courtship dance has all the passion of a tango. It marks a mutual understanding between the birds. Once bonded, breeding may begin.

Today, grebes are common on lakes and waterways across Europe. But in the 1800s they were hunted in Britain to the point of near extinction, as their feathers were much sought after by the fashion trade. In 1889 two far-sighted women realised that these birds were imperilled and they formed what became the Royal Society for the Protection of Birds (RSPB), one of the most influential conservation organisations.

The most aquatic of birds, grebes never come to land. They build floating nests and carry their stripy young on their backs. Romantic dancers and attentive parents, once the breeding season is over, they moult to reveal less fancy garb. Winter is spent at the coast, but come spring, they will be 'dressing to impress' again, ready to charm a new partner.

'crrrahrrr...'

They are known in the UK as the car goose and diver doucker.

- **IUCN status:** Least Concern
- **UK status:** Green
- **Length:** 50 cm
- **Wingspan:** 72 cm
- **Visible:** All year
- **Sexes:** Alike
- **Voice:** Highly vocal. Loud, strong 'crrrahrrr' and 'vrekk-vrekk-vrekk' during display.

'srih-srih-srih

srih-srih-srih

srih-srih-srih'

In the UK, they
are sometimes called
the creak-mouse.

- **IUCN status:** Least Concern
- **UK status:** Green
- **Length:** 14 cm
- **Wingspan:** 18 cm
- **Visible:** All year
- **Sexes:** Alike
- **Voice:** Chatty, clicking calls, 'si-si-si'.
  Short, high-pitched 'srih-srih-srih'.

LONG-TAILED TIT
AEGITHALOS CAUDATUS

Sunlight glints on frost as you walk beside the hedgerow, the park still and quiet. Over the top of the hawthorn comes a twittering flock of tiny birds. Deep in conversation, they are unworried by your presence as they feed together on a cherry tree. This is a group of long-tailed tits. They are exquisite pink and grey pom-poms with delicate tails far longer than their bodies.

In winter, LTTs, as they're known, move around in flocks of up to twenty birds. These are extended families of parents, offspring and other close relatives. Their non-stop calls help the group remain together while each bird searches for insects and other invertebrates. These are family-minded 'home birds', they will help raise each other's young in spring and, in the darker months, they stay close together for survival. Left alone, a long-tailed tit could die on a wintery night. Instead, these birds find shelter in shrubs and sleep snuggled close together.

The population of these distinctive little birds is growing faster in parks than in their traditional woodlands, possibly due to the warmer nights in built-up areas.

LTTs are skilled architects. They rear their chicks in one of the most intricate and beautiful nests in the bird world. They collect around 3,000 specks of moss and feathers and bind them together with strands of spiders' web to build a domed cave. This camouflaged nest is difficult to find. The entrance is placed cleverly at the side to keep out the rain. LTTs have large families, sometimes up to twelve chicks.

Cooperative, busy and chattering, these dapper birds are a highlight of our parks. Their welcoming 'si-si-si-si' calls, best remembered as 'ease-ease-ease', can help us weather the darker days until spring returns.

COLLARED DOVE
STREPTOPELIA DECAOCTO

The soothing 'good morn-ning, good morn-ning' of the collared dove often welcomes us to the park. Their subtle, sandy, pinkish-grey plumage with black-on-white collar makes them easy to spot. The sexes are alike but the young lack the neckband. They are frequent visitors to our gardens and at first glance they seem to be cosy, homely birds. But the history of the dove tells a different story: these are mysterious adventurers with 'itchy' wings!

In the 1800s, collared doves were confined to Turkey and western Asia. Then, inexplicably, in the space of just 100 years, they appeared over most of Europe, where they stayed. They first bred in Britain in 1955 and were a star attraction for birders. Britain has almost a million pairs today. We don't understand what triggered this expansion, and dove numbers appear to have been stable for years before their European colonisation. One theory is that the birds experienced a random genetic mutation that shifted their behaviour, but the evidence for this idea is so far inconclusive.

One of the reasons for the doves' success is their extraordinary breeding rate. They can produce up to five broods in a year. They usually choose to nest close to humans, in parks and suburbia. Their nests are loose platforms made from twigs, often placed in a fork of branches, or even on the brackets of satellite dishes. Doves feed almost exclusively on seeds and grain, but occasionally take invertebrates, and often visit bird tables.

Behind their stay-at-home exterior, these birds have wanderlust and a taste for the open skies. Young have been known to travel an extraordinary 600 kilometres away from their hatching place.

'do dooo do do dooo do do dooo do do dooo do do dooo do do dooo do'

In Germany they are known as television doves.

- **IUCN status:** Least Concern
- **UK status:** Green
- **Length:** 32 cm
- **Wingspan:** 55 cm
- **Visible:** All year

- **Sexes:** Alike
- **Voice:** Soft cooing three-note call, 'do dooo do'. Mnemonic for call is 'good morn-ning, good morn-ning'.

- **IUCN status:** Least Concern
- **UK status:** Green
- **Length:** 45 cm
- **Wingspan:** 56 cm
- **Visible:** All year
- **Sexes:** Alike
- **Voice:** Scratchy, chattering. Alarm call is 'tsche tsche tsche'.

'tsche tsche tsche'

Local names in the UK include pie and chattermag.

MAGPIE
PICA PICA

Masterminds or master villains? Magpies are easy to identify. Their long tails and distinctive black, white and iridescent purple and green plumage make them stand out from the crowd. They are often portrayed as the baddies of the bird world: the killers who devour nestlings and eggs. In reality, they are no more predatory than great spotted woodpeckers.

Their diet in winter is largely vegetarian and in summer they eat mostly invertebrates. Only in spring do they target nestlings as part of their diet. Both sexes and their young are similar, although juveniles have shorter tails.

Magpies are members of the corvid, or crow, family. They are not only one of the most intelligent birds in the world but are one of the brightest of all animals. They have numerical abilities and can even recognise themselves in mirrors, which suggests that they have self-awareness.

Magpies appear in songs, myths and superstitions. Sometimes as a wise friend; sometimes a dangerous thief. Much of our mistrust of magpies and their

kin comes from their historical habit of scavenging from dead bodies. They used to appear on battlefields to exploit the feast. This made magpies creatures of ill-omen in some European folklore. Like all crows, they used their keen eyesight and intelligence to take advantage of a new feeding opportunity, which is why they have now moved into towns.

These arch-recyclers consume food scraps and roadkill. Their role is similar to that of vultures in Africa who strip carcasses and keep the savannah free of disease. Without the magpies' enthusiasm for eating carrion, our city parks and streets would be much less healthy environments for us.

SWIFT
APUS APUS

Often heard before they are seen, the swifts' piercing scream announces that summer is almost here. The crescent-shaped wings of these urban migrants are distinctive as they scud over the rooftops in May.

Adult swifts rarely come to land, and they fly non-stop for ten months of the year. They feed, mate and sleep on the wing. Even nesting material is plucked from the air mid-flight. Their scientific name, *Apus*, means 'no feet' because their legs are rarely seen. Swifts pair for life and return to the same nest site annually. They breed as a colony, tucked up in holes and gaps under eaves or in the walls of buildings. One colony in Scotland does things a little differently: it nests in trees, as the swifts' ancestors would have done, by repurposing disused woodpecker nests.

Once breeding is complete, around August, the swifts speed away to sub-Saharan Africa. Swifts are well-named, as they are daring aerialists. But they also deserve their older names of devil birds or screamers. At dusk the birds drop from their rooftop nests to feed, darting around the sky with mouths open to sweep up the 10,000 flying insects and tiny windborne spiderlings that make up their daily diet. It is then that they make their shrill, penetrating calls. Although swifts appear to be related to swallows, there is no genetic connection there, and their closest living relatives are in fact hummingbirds.

Swifts welcome new breeding sites in towns, and we can invite them in by adding nest boxes to the eaves of our houses. They are mysterious birds and are difficult to study, as much of their life remains hidden from view – all but for a few months when they dance into our skies.

'srriiirr'

'srriiirr'

'srriiirr'

In England they are sometimes known as devil birds or screamers.

- **IUCN status:** Least Concern
- **UK status:** Amber
- **Length:** 17 cm
- **Wingspan:** 45 cm

- **Visible:** April to August
- **Sexes:** Alike
- **Voice:** Shrill calls.
  Chorus of screams: 'srriiirr'.

'zi-zee-litt'

'zi-zee-litt'

In Somerset they are known as dish-dashers, and in Cheshire, England, water wagtails.

- **IUCN status:** Least Concern
- **UK status:** Green
- **Length:** 17 cm
- **Wingspan:** 29 cm

- **Visible:** All year
- **Sexes:** Alike
- **Voice:** High pitched and rapid chattering, 'chis-ick' or 'zi-zee-litt'.

PIED WAGTAIL
MOTACILLA ALBA

The sprightly pied wagtail rarely walks. Instead, it sprints everywhere on legs that seem powered by clockwork. Even when standing still, its long tail wags and bobs ceaselessly. These birds fly well, and during the colder months they gather in large flocks at dusk in the city to roost, making their loud and sweet two- or three-note call. For the rest of the year, they spend most of their time on the ground, alone or in pairs. They are quite socially intolerant of other birds.

Wagtails were originally birds of meadows and open countryside, but many have made the move to city life and they can often be spotted hurrying around shopping centre car parks, service stations and playgrounds in search of insects. At night they favour areas illuminated by neon lighting, which may help deter their predators.

Male and female wagtails are very similar, although the male has a much darker back than the female. They nest underneath eaves or in gaps in walls where bricks are missing – sites that are often available in cities. Urban gardeners can help wagtails by installing open-fronted nest boxes about two metres off the ground, out of direct sunlight. Both sexes are territorial in spring and pied wagtails have been seen attacking car side-mirrors when they catch sight of their own reflection. The call of the pied wagtail is 'chis-ick', with the emphasis on the second syllable. In London, they're known as 'the Chiswick Flyover', after one of the main roads to the city.

Throughout much of Europe, the pied wagtail is replaced by the white wagtail. This is a form of the same species. Their habits and lifestyle remain the same, but they have a grey rather than black back.

CITY PIGEONS
COLUMBA LIVIA DOMESTICA

At sunrise, against a sky streaked with orange and mauve, on an unseen cue, a flight of pigeons leaves its rooftop roost and breaks into the air. The birds circle once, twice, then glide to the ground.

Too often, city pigeons get a bad press. In fact, they were Charles Darwin's favourite bird and have saved lives carrying messages during times of war – they are one of the most important birds in the history of human survival.

Their story begins 10,000 years ago. Young rock doves, a species that lives around cliffs and rocky outcrops, were reared by humans for food. Many birds escaped captivity and searched for suitable sites to live in. Wild rock doves build their nests on cliff face ledges, and tall town buildings with windowsills and rooftops offer excellent alternatives. Rock doves feed on seeds and grain, while city pigeons have a broader diet that includes the leftovers of human food.

Pigeons can be seen in a variety of smoky and earthy shades: blues, greys, blacks, browns and brick-reds. They may have a chequered pattern on their wings, and purple, pink or green hues on their necks. Sexes are similar and mate for life. For two months, their young, or 'squabs', are fed milk by both parents. Pigeon 'milk' is produced in the crop; an area between their throat and stomach.

These are 'home birds', despite their navigational ability. Pigeon races still take place: pigeons fly between 100 and 1,000 kilometres before returning to their loft. This reveals the strong bond between pigeons and places. These loyal birds are symbols of love in many cultures and their cooing is a sound that people have known since ancient times.

'coo... coo'

'look-at-the-moon'

In the UK they are also known as street pigeons, city doves and feral pigeons.

- **IUCN status:** Least Concern
- **UK status:** Green
- **Length:** 33 cm
- **Wingspan:** 66 cm
- **Visible:** All year
- **Sexes:** Alike
- **Voice:** Soft, continuous 'coo'. Mnemonic for their coo is 'look-at-the moon'.

- **IUCN status:** Least Concern
- **UK status:** Green
- **Length:** 28 cm
- **Wingspan:** 36 cm

- **Visible:** All year
- **Sexes:** Differ, see opposite
- **Voice:** Ranging from melodious flute-like song to harsh clacking 'pli-pli-pli-pli'.

They can be called the merle in Scotland and colly in England (a dialect word for black).

'pli-pli-pli-pli'

'pli-pli-pli-pli'

'pli-pli-pli-pli'

'pli-pli-pli-pli'

BLACKBIRD
TURDUS MERULA

Blackbirds are our buskers, the street singers who put smiles on our faces as we go about our lives. Often the first and last to sing each day, blackbirds are one of the stars in spring's dawn chorus. But equally, at dusk on a cold winter evening, their bright and melodious song lifts our spirits. The male's flute-like phrases are warm and friendly. He sings from a perch just above our heads, almost within reach.

Blackbirds are one of the very few birds that sing at night, particularly in cities where streetlights lengthen the natural day. City blackbirds appear to build their nests as close as possible to light sources, maybe because they can then feed for longer on dark days. Research shows that urban blackbirds have a longer lifespan than their rural cousins.

It is the male, ebony coloured with a yellow beak and eye-ring, who sings. The female and juvenile are both soft-brown in plumage. Surprisingly, white blackbirds are not uncommon. This colour variation is often only partial, so it is possible to see blackbirds with a white tail or half-wing. Every winter, large numbers of blackbirds travel south to avoid the cold weather in Scandinavia, where deep snow hides their food of earthworms, insects and berries. This influx of migrants is one of the reasons that resident blackbirds sing all year round. Their territorial 'mik-mik' call alerts potential intruders that a patch is already taken.

Blackbirds were once shy woodlanders who carefully avoided humans. But, as cities grew, blackbirds adapted. Over the past hundred years they have become confident with people and can now be found in every town and city, making this bird one of our most popular wild companions.

HOUSE SPARROW
PASSER DOMESTICUS

Cheeky, chirpy and a skilled survivor, no bird has a longer history of living alongside the people of Europe than the ingenious house sparrow. Sparrows made the journey north with our prehistoric ancestors. They thrived alongside early farmers and fed on farmland. They have even been known to live deep in a coal mine or indoors at an airport terminal.

Large flocks once lived in almost every town and village. As humans migrated into cities, sparrows followed. Until recently, these birds were so numerous that they were a source of food for people across Europe. Sparrow pie was popular. But over the past fifty years, more than seventy percent of them have disappeared. They are not an endangered species globally, but sparrows are becoming an unusual sight in city centres. Pollution, domestic cats and disease are just a few of the possible causes for their decline – avian malaria being the most likely culprit.

Sparrows are snappy dressers. In spring, the male has a chestnut coloured back and a smart black bib: the bigger the bib, the higher his status. His female mate sports plumage in subtle shades of brown all year round. House sparrows are assertive and territorial. As colony nesters, they may attack and even kill other species that attempt to share their habitat. This is one of the keys to their success: they remove competition for food and nest sites. Pairs of sparrows are not always faithful. DNA tests have confirmed that fifteen percent of offspring are the result of mating outside of an established coupling.

Sparrows are enthusiastic bathers, in either water or dust. They can often be spotted in roadside puddles, and dust baths keep away parasites and remove excess oil from their feathers.

- **IUCN status:** Least Concern
- **UK status:** Red
- **Length:** 15 cm
- **Wingspan:** 23 cm
- **Visible:** All year

- **Sexes:** Differ, see opposite
- **Voice:** Short cheeps and incessant chirps. Double note 'philip' call. When annoyed, 'cher–r-r-r-r'.

'philip'   'philip'

Local names in England
include sparr, spadger,
spadgick, Philip
and spuggy.

In Scotland they are
called the stuckie,
and in Wales,
bird of the snow.

- **IUCN status:** Least Concern
- **UK status:** Red
- **Length:** 21 cm
- **Wingspan:** 40 cm
- **Visible:** All year
- **Sexes:** Alike
- **Voice:** Wide range of whistles and clicks.

STARLING
STURNUS VULGARIS

Starlings are great illusionists. At a distance, they look black, but up close, their glossy plumage is cream-speckled with a sheen of green and purple. Multi-talented starlings are full of surprises.

Many birds produce just one or two songs, but starlings shriek, chatter, chirp and purr. They are excellent mimics and can reproduce calls of more than twenty other species. They also copy a whole range of inanimate sounds. Ringtones, car alarms, police sirens – all of these form part of their repertoire, which can make it a challenge to identify them!

The starling offers yet another surprise. In midwinter, flocks of more than one million birds roost at a range of locations. In city squares, railway stations, seaside piers, woodlands or reed beds, these cold-weather gatherings produce a memorable sight: the murmuration. At dusk, before coming in to roost, huge groups of starlings swirl, swoop and sweep around the sky. They move together in a complex choreography that science doesn't yet fully understand. From a distance the flocks look like clouds of smoke, twisting in the wind. Viewing them from a little closer, the display seems to be a well-rehearsed *corps de ballet*. The spectacle continues until they drop down onto buildings or trees at nightfall.

Starlings live and feed alongside us. Using sharp probing beaks, they search for insects, seeds and food scraps. But they have one more surprise in store. While sexes are alike, young starlings are brown-grey in plumage and look so different from their parents that it is easy to think they are a separate species. Nothing is as it seems with these exquisite fliers. They fill our winter months with a mystery of their own.

RING-NECKED PARAKEET

PSITTACULA KRAMERI

You see a flash of brilliant green and a raucous chattering in the treetops. Did you have one too many espressos this morning or was that really a flock, or 'pandemonium', of city-dwelling parrots?

Some birds have the ability to carry you away from the concrete jungle to exotic forests. Originally from a tropical belt spanning west Africa to lowland India, ring-necked, or rose-ringed, parakeets are named after the distinctive black and pink necklace sported by the male – missing from the female. Historically, millions were sold as pets around the world. Many escaped and learned to survive in new habitats. As Europe's first naturalised parrot, visitors to a growing list of cities are surprised by the emerald green parakeets prattling in the trees.

They are hole nesters, laying their eggs in hollow trees or inside buildings. They are not always easy to spot, as their feathers are camouflaged against the lighter leaves. But they are unmistakable when they call. They have strong voices and are vocal in flight. This can make them unpopular when they visit bird tables in the morning.

Parakeets dine on seeds, fruit and berries, and often leave urban areas to feed in nearby farmland. They return to town at nightfall to take advantage of this heat island. A city centre can be 5°C warmer than the surrounding countryside as built-up areas generate huge amounts of heat from cars, houses, factories and shops.

Despite their appeal, parakeets are something of a problem. There are concerns about their impact on native wildlife and commercial orchards. Cities have few predators and parakeets have little competition from other birds, so the population is steadily increasing.

'kyiik kyiik kyiik'.

- ■ **IUCN status:** Least Concern
- ■ **UK status:** Introduced
- ■ **Length:** 40 cm
- ■ **Wingspan:** 45 cm
- ■ **Visible:** All year
- ■ **Sexes:** Differ, see opposite
- ■ **Voice:** Shrill screech, 'kyiik kyiik kyiik'.

In Scotland these are known as
water blackbirds and river pies,
and as water crows in Ireland.

'stretts stretts'

- **IUCN status:** Least Concern
- **UK status:** Amber
- **Length:** 18 cm
- **Wingspan:** 28 cm

- **Visible:** All year
- **Sexes:** Alike
- **Voice:** Song is alternating soft and harsh throaty notes. The call is short 'stretts'.

DIPPER
CINCLUS CINCLUS

Mid-winter, walking by a fast-flowing river, you may hear a loud, babbling song before spotting a plump bird moving up and down on a boulder mid-stream. Named after that bobbing motion, this is the dipper.

These are early breeders, and the male dipper sings to establish his territory. His voice is high-pitched and metallic. Bobbing in his smart 'tuxedo' plumage with black-brown feathers, a white bib and a short, cocked tail, this bird isn't difficult to identify. The young are grey with a white bib. Dippers have the basic body shape of an adult wren.

Dippers call from a rock perch mid-stream before slipping into the torrent. Completely submerged, with the aid of their wings, they walk – or 'fly' – underwater. They head upstream holding on to the riverbed with powerful feet. Their sharp beaks probe aquatic plants and turn over small stones, under which they find creatures, such as young fish and larvae, to eat. After twenty seconds they emerge.

Dippers fly in short bursts, keeping low over the water, always following the path of the river. They are perfectly adapted to their specialised life. They have flaps over their nostrils that snap shut underwater, and they close a semi-transparent third eyelid, which protects the eyes, but allows them to see as they swim. Dippers use their beaks to take oil from a gland at the base of the tail and to work it into their feathers. This provides a waterproof coating that prevents the chill of the water coming into contact with their skin.

Dippers thrive in fast-flowing waters. They're loyal to these locations and some of their nest sites have been in use for more than 120 years. These birds are the beating heart of upland streams.

MALLARD
ANAS PLATYRHYNCHOS

As a winter wind blows and you pull your scarf closer, the jostling flock of noisy birds at your feet eating grain are likely to be mallards – familiar, yet full of surprises.

Some of the birds you feed in your local park during the darker months may, in fact, have travelled from as far away as Russia! During autumn and winter, migrant ducks join our resident flocks in large numbers. Males are flamboyant with their iridescent, metallic-green heads, thin, white necklaces and yellow beaks. Both sexes have a flash of blue on their wings. Females incubate their eggs without help from their mate, and their subtle, mottled brown plumage and dark beaks are excellent camouflage among vegetation.

Mallards are dabbling ducks which means that they feed on the surface of the water or just beneath. They are the ancestors of most domestic breeds. It is only females that produce the raucous 'quack'.

As highly sociable ducks, mallards are never far from others of their kind. However, in summer, males perform an extraordinary disappearing trick. In the space of a few weeks, flocks seem to be composed of females only. This is an illusion: the males are present, but are in 'eclipse plumage'. This phenomenon occurs after breeding, when the males need to moult their worn feathers. The birds are flightless at this time, and very vulnerable to predators, so they develop a brown plumage similar to the females' camouflage. By the end of summer, their normal feathers grow back, and the colourful male mallards reappear.

These are often among the first birds we come to know, and these resilient, adaptable illusionists introduce us to the world of wild birds.

'creak'

The female is brown, with dark mottling and a eyestripe, lacking the metallic green head and white necklace.

'quack!'

In Scotland they can be called moss ducks.

- **IUCN status:** Least Concern
- **UK status:** Green
- **Length:** 62 cm
- **Wingspan:** 95 cm

- **Visible:** All year
- **Sexes:** Differ, see opposite
- **Voice:** Males give a rasping creak, females give a loud 'quack'.

'zi zi'

'zi zi'

'zi zi'

'zi zi'

In southeast England
they can be called
water wagtails.

- **IUCN status:** Least Concern
- **UK status:** Red
- **Length:** 20 cm
- **Wingspan:** 26 cm

- **Visible:** All year
- **Sexes:** Differ, see opposite
- **Voice:** Call is a sharp, penetrating 'zi zi'. The song is short and sharp.

GREY WAGTAIL
MOTACILLA CINEREA

During mid-summer, you may spot a grey wagtail flitting elegantly over a stream from its nest in the wall of an old stone bridge. One, then another, will perch on the pebbled waterline before darting up to snatch a meal for their chicks. Charming and delicate, these birds occupy the most photogenic locations.

Despite their name, a fast-moving streak of sunshine-yellow is the best way to identify these birds as they patrol riverbanks and streams. Although yellow covers only the chest and underside; their smoke-grey upper feathers are often hidden against the water. The sexes are very similar, but the males have a larger, brighter patch of yellow on their undersides and, in spring, sport an elegant black bib on their throats. Both sexes flick their long tails continually.

Grey wagtails feed on ants when on grassland, catch midges and flies in mid-air, and grab the occasional unwary tadpole from shallow water. They rarely fly in a straight line. They dart off at an angle having spotted something interesting to eat. Like all wagtails,

they spend a lot of time on the ground. As pollution levels in many of Europe's waterways have decreased, grey wagtail numbers have slowly increased. They were once confined mainly to fast-flowing hill streams, but they can now be seen on farmland and canal banks.

In winter, when weather in the uplands becomes too harsh, wagtails often move down to lower altitudes. Some have even been recorded in towns and cities where they can still find their insect prey during warmer winter temperatures. Swift and subtle, with a high-pitched call, grey wagtails have a grace all of their own.

KINGFISHER
ALCEDO ATTHIS

As you slip your canoe into the water and paddle silently, you may see an electric-blue dot on a branch ahead. Slowly, the current takes you closer, and the dot transforms into a lightning flash of blue. This is a kingfisher. It darts forward, down into the water and off again.

A kingfisher streaking low over water is one of the most breathtaking sights of a day spent by the river. Look carefully and you might find the bird's hunting perch – a thin, overhanging branch where it will watch until a stickleback or minnow swims into view. The kingfisher will first bob its head up and down, judging the exact position of its prey, before performing a power-dive into the water. With its wings folded back, its aerodynamic body barely makes a splash as it disappears from view. If you (and the kingfisher) are lucky, a few seconds later it will emerge with a wriggling fish in its beak.

Having such short wings, the kingfisher's fast flight uses a lot of energy, and this bird needs to eat up to sixty percent of its own bodyweight each day. The sexes are similar; the male has an all-black beak,

while the bottom half of the female's beak is orange. A pair of kingfishers will nest in a tunnel they excavated themselves. They start by drilling a hole in a sandy bank. Next, they dig a passage that slopes slightly upwards to keep out the rain. At the end of the passage is a small, round chamber that will be home to their chicks.

Most kingfishers live for a year only. Vivid and all-too-brief, a sighting leaves an emotional afterglow. But a flight that seems effortless conceals the fiery energy needed to keep such a small bird safe against the perils of drought, flood, ice and snow.

'zii   zii   ti'

In England they
are often known
as fishers.

- **IUCN status:** Least Concern
- **UK status:** Amber
- **Length:** 16 cm
- **Wingspan:** 25 cm

- **Visible:** All year
- **Sexes:** Alike
- **Voice:** Call is a high-pitched, sharp, whistled 'zii zii ti'.

In the UK they are also known as fishing eagles or fish hawks.

'kew
  kew
    kew'

'kew kew kew'

- **IUCN status:** Least Concern
- **UK status:** Amber
- **Length:** 60 cm
- **Wingspan:** 170 cm

- **Visible:** March to October
- **Sexes:** Alike
- **Voice:** Display call is a mournful whistle. Alarm call is 'kew kew kew'.

OSPREY
PANDION HALIAETUS

On a bright morning, you may spot an osprey swooping low over sparkling water, plunging its talons beneath the surface to emerge, in a shower of glittering spray, carrying a salmon.

Ospreys are specialised hunters. They snatch small fish from the water mid-flight – although heavier prey does bring this bird crashing into the lake! Their legs are long and featherless, to prevent them becoming too waterlogged for flight. Their feet are equipped with sharp talons surrounded by tough, fleshy spines – essential when holding on to wriggling fish. Brown above and white below, the osprey's long, thin wings and short tail make it distinctive and easy to identify.

The famous ospreys of Loch Garten in Scotland were one of the world's first examples of 'conservation tourism'. Operation Osprey was established in 1959 to protect the nests of the recolonising birds. People were invited to view the birds' courtship rituals and sky-dances. Osprey pairs mate for life and are loyal to their nesting sites, which are usually found at the top of a tall tree or a manmade structure, such as a pylon, transmission tower or purpose-built platform. Throughout Europe, ospreys were threatened until recently. Their numbers have increased during the last sixty years and are growing.

Ospreys visit the northern hemisphere for the breeding season only. They spend their winters in west Africa. Ospreys can be seen hunting almost anywhere in Europe during spring and autumn as they migrate. Keep an eye on reservoirs, lakes and other unpolluted stretches of water. Elegant and dramatic, these exquisite birds bring a little African sunshine to our summer skies.

GREY HERON
ARDEA CINEREA

A little after sunrise, you may see the glassy surface of a lake broken by an eerie watcher. A head moves forwards almost imperceptibly as a step is taken. Next, you might glimpse a flash of rapier beak and a silver fish before the prey is swallowed whole. Then the bird is still again.

The grey heron is one of Europe's tallest birds. Both sexes are alike, and adults weigh less than two kilograms. They are slender and almost invisible among reeds. This is an important part of their feeding strategy – herons are skilled at the waiting game. They stand in shallow water, still and silent, before their beaks dart down to snatch prey.

In flight, herons appear prehistoric – more pterodactyl-like than bird-like. Their immense, slow-beating wings can be seen from a great distance. Their long legs trail behind, and their thin neck is pulled back into a distinctive S-shape.

Herons were once timid creatures. They were driven off or killed by landowners with fish to protect. For centuries, they were also hunted for food, and were a highlight on dining tables of the wealthy. Herons are legally protected now. They are adapting to their new sense of safety and have become more approachable in our urban waterways. Today, their real enemy is a bad winter. When lakes and ponds freeze over, their food becomes trapped. Thousands of herons risk starvation when temperatures hit sub-zero for more than a few days.

At the lake, high among the branches, you may see large twig-nests. This is a heronry: the breeding colony of the birds. When they are all together, the noise of their throaty croak sounds almost as ancient as the herons appear in flight.

'craaahnk'

Also known in the
UK as a harn, hernser
and hernshaw, and
as a hragra in
traditional English.

- **IUCN status:** Least Concern
- **UK status:** Green
- **Length:** 95 cm
- **Wingspan:** 180 cm

- **Visible:** All year
- **Sexes:** Alike
- **Voice:** Call is loud, harsh, slow 'craaahnk'.

- **IUCN status:** Near Threatened
- **UK status:** Green
- **Length:** 64 cm
- **Wingspan:** 185 cm
- **Visible:** All year
- **Sexes:** Alike
- **Voice:** Their display call is a high-pitched mewing.

'weee–ooo ee oo ee oo ee oo'

'weee–ooo ee oo ee oo ee oo'

RED KITE
MILVUS MILVUS

These elegant birds of prey soar above the countryside with loud, high-pitched mewing calls. Being unusually sociable for raptors, they often fly in groups, and make a haunting spectacle as they come into their woodland roosts. Their pale heads, reddish-brown bodies, angled wings and forked tails make them unmistakable.

Large populations of red kites can be seen in Germany, France and Spain. In the UK, these magnificent birds were on the brink of extinction by the 1930s and were confined to Wales. But, after a successful reintroduction scheme and an outstanding conservation effort, their range is now once again increasing. One of the best places in Europe to spot these balletic birds is from the M40 motorway between Oxford and London, as they ride on the warm thermals created by the traffic below!

Red kites mate for life, returning to the same nest site each year between March and May to breed. They construct their nests with twigs and mud, and, taking advantage of their farmland neighbours, they line the nests with sheep's wool

for added warmth. These birds are also attracted to colourful objects, which can sometimes make it into their nests. A toy giraffe, handbags, a teddy bear and socks have all been scavenged by the birds.

The male journeys to and from the nest, bringing food for his mate who is patiently incubating their eggs. Carrion and worms form the bulk of their diet, but as opportunistic feeders, they will occasionally swoop to catch small mammals, such as mice, shrews, voles and young rabbits. In some parts of Europe, people attract kites to their gardens, stocking a raptor bird table with scraps from the local butcher.

BARN OWL
TYTO ALBA

During a winter evening, as frosty grass crunches beneath your boots and the sun sets ahead, you may notice a glimpse of white. It is the buoyant, 'floating' flight of a barn owl hunting low over the ground.

These much-loved countryside birds can be seen across most of Europe. They have white faces with dark eyes, a smooth rounded head without ear tufts, a mottled grey-and-buff back and ghostly white underparts.

They are often most active shortly before dusk, but when food is scarce, they will also hunt during the daytime. Their heart-shaped faces help them locate prey: the concave shape directs high-frequency sounds to their ears, which are at different heights on either side of their head. The owl can then pinpoint scuttling voles and shrews. Tiny serrations on the edges of their flight feathers break up the flow of air over their wings, enabling them to glide silently towards a target meal. The owl will pause, hovering over the prey for a brief moment, then swoop down to grab the vole with its talons before swallowing it whole.

In late winter, barn owl pairs preen each other and rub their cheeks together in courtship. In early spring the pair will nest, often in an old farm building. If none is available, they will find a cavity in a tree or cliff face.

They often lay their eggs on a layer of compacted 'pellets': small parcels of undigested food regurgitated by females. The male will bring food to the female and young until the chicks are three weeks old, then the female joins the hunt. Their silent flight and unearthly shrieking call has given owls an unfortunate association with approaching death or bad luck in many cultures.

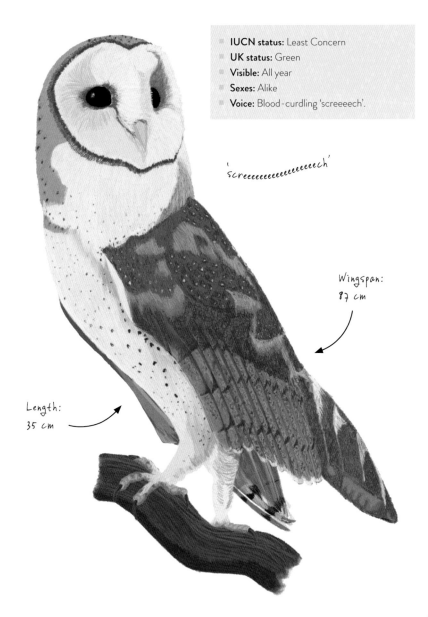

IUCN status: Least Concern
UK status: Green
Visible: All year
Sexes: Alike
Voice: Blood-curdling 'screeeech'.

'screeeeeeeeeeeeeeeeeech'

Wingspan:
87 cm

Length:
35 cm

- **IUCN status:** Near Threatened
- **UK status:** Red
- **Length:** 30 cm
- **Wingspan:** 85 cm
- **Visible:** All year
- **Sexes:** Alike
- **Voice:** Call is a 'peewit'. Song is 'pee-wit wit wit-eeze wit'.

'pee-wit wit wit-eeze wit'

Local names for the Lapwing include peewit in Europe, and green plover in England and Ireland.

LAPWING
VANELLUS VANELLUS

The lapwings' mournful, haunting 'pee-wit' call is a familiar farmland sound. These are birds guided by the weather in their hunt for the invertebrates that form their diet.

In autumn, southern flocks swell with birds escaping the cold of northern Europe, as they land on lowland pasture. In extremely frosty conditions, migrants may continue their journey south until they reach France or Spain. Even during these cold years, they will return north at the onset of spring. It is during this season that we witness the males' iconic, piercing calls and tumbling aerial displays; consisting of zigzagging flight, rolls and dives through the air.

Its splendid crest makes the lapwing stand out – look for this if you see a group of birds on a ploughed field. Males have a slightly longer crest than females. The rest of their body is black and white, with tinted green feathers on their backs. The birds' scientific name *Vanellus* means 'little fan' and refers to the rapid motion of their wings.

Breeding lapwings make simple nests in open countryside by digging shallow scrapes into the ground. Laying eggs here is risky, so eggshells are patterned with camouflage for safety. If a predator, such as a fox or crow, ventures too close, lapwing parents will fly at the intruder in defence to distract them from the nest.

Soon after the eggs hatch, a family of lapwings will move on, and the fluffy chicks will begin to forage. This is something you can spy from afar through a pair of binoculars. Historically, lapwing eggs were considered an expensive delicacy, and searching for them in springtime led to the modern-day Easter egg hunt!

YELLOWHAMMER
EMBERIZA CITRINELLA

Climbing over a stile into a field, you may hear a distinctive call: a rhythmic series of short notes, getting louder, as a male yellowhammer perched in a bush projects his 'little bit of bread and no cheeeeese' song. Each bird learns the song from its father, so these birds sing with regional accents passed down through generations!

Following the song will guide you to the bird's location. Males are unmistakeable – especially in their breeding plumage – with a vibrant yellow head and underparts, a streaked brown-black back and a chestnut rump. Females are duller in colour and their feathers are more mottled on their crown, breast and flanks.

At the start of the breeding season in May, a male raises his wings and runs towards a female – if you watch quietly, you may be lucky enough to see this comical display. After pairing up, female yellowhammers find a well-hidden spot on or near to the ground where they construct a lined, cup-shape nest from grass and moss. Females will lay between two and six eggs, which are patterned with a mesh of fine, dark lines. It is these lines that gave the bird its Old English name of the scribble lark.

Outside of breeding season, yellowhammers form large flocks that feed together on mixed arable and livestock farmland – a memorable sight for any bird enthusiast.

Their bright-yellow colour fades slightly during the winter. Their diet during this part of the year is made up of seeds, cereals and grains, rather than the rich caterpillars, worms and spiders enjoyed during spring. They find it harder to obtain food over the cold months, so if you have a rural garden, tempt them in with seeds.

'si-si-si-si-suu'

This bird is known as the yellow yorling in Northern Ireland, Scotland and northern England.

- **IUCN status:** Least Concern
- **UK status:** Red
- **Length:** 16 cm
- **Wingspan:** 25 cm

- **Visible:** All year
- **Sexes:** Differ, see opposite
- **Voice:** High-pitched song. Call is short, stifled, 'si-si-si-si-suu'.

- **IUCN status:** Least Concern
- **UK status:** Amber
- **Length:** 33 cm
- **Wingspan:** 76 cm
- **Visible:** All year
- **Sexes:** Differ, see opposite
- **Voice:** Call is a loud, shrill 'kee-kee-kee'.

'kee-kee-kee...'   '...kee-kee-kee'

Their aerial prowess
has given them the
alternative name
windhover
in the UK.

KESTREL
FALCO TINNUNCULUS

While driving along a motorway you may notice a bird with pointed wings and a long, fan-shaped tail hovering above the roadside. This is a kestrel, using its razor-sharp vision to hunt for a vole, waiting for the perfect moment to pounce. Kestrels can see ultraviolet light, meaning they can detect the luminous urine trails left by rodents. They follow these along the ground, straight to their prey.

While other birds of prey are capable of hovering for a few seconds, the kestrel is the true master of this skill. It is the birds' main hunting method, and it has resulted in them being given the evocative name of windhovers in the UK. If you can catch a glimpse of a hovering kestrel through a pair of binoculars, you will notice the head stays perfectly still, as their eyes focus on the grass below: a technique which increases their hunting ability tenfold. Making subtle adjustments with its tail, it barely needs to beat its wings as it faces into the wind.

Unlike most raptors, male and female kestrels have different colouration. The male has a grey-blue head and tail, with fewer black spots and streaks across its body. The female is entirely brown and is larger than the male.

Changes in agricultural practices have caused the population of the kestrels' field vole prey to decline and have also reduced the number of nest sites, so kestrel numbers have decreased since the 1970s. But, this resilient bird of prey has adapted well to man-made environments, and can survive within the hustle and bustle of a metropolis, so there is a chance you could spot one while strolling through the city.

BUZZARD
BUTEO BUTEO

On a clear day, you may well spot this regal, brown bird, with its short, powerful neck and rounded wings held in a V-shape, wheeling through the skies in search of food far below on the ground. The buzzard is probably the most common bird of prey in Europe, and numbers have quadrupled since 1970.

You will often see this bird in a tree or on top of a fence post. Buzzards spend most of their days on their perch, which has given them a reputation for being sluggish. This is why they have never been popular with falconers: it is believed that they are unwilling to chase live prey, as a falconer's bird needs to do. However, they are in fact cleverly conserving energy. The buzzard will wait on his perch, scouring the ground for movement – such as a disruption in the soil where a vole is moving underneath – before taking flight to capture the prey. This hunt does not always take place though, as a large part of the buzzard's diet is made up of carrion and earthworms.

The best time to go buzzard-spotting is in early spring, when males put on acrobatic aerial displays to impress females. They fly up high before plummeting downwards in twists and turns as if on a rollercoaster. After forming a lifelong bond, a buzzard pair will fiercely defend their territory from intruders. It is here that they will nest and raise their young – something which now occurs in every European country except for Iceland.

The increase in buzzard numbers is largely due to the control of pesticide use, in particular the banning of DDT. This chemical thinned their eggshells, so few of the young hatched. This turnabout in fortunes shows how quickly populations can recover with a little care.

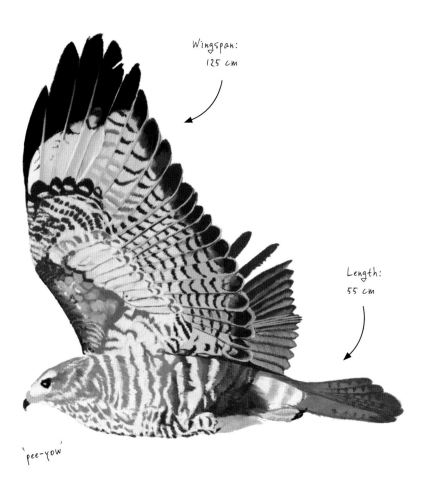

Wingspan:
125 cm

Length:
55 cm

'pee-yow'

- **IUCN status:** Least Concern
- **UK status:** Green
- **Visible:** All year

- **Sexes:** Alike
- **Voice:** Loud, drawn-out, high-pitched, 'pee-yow' call.

Puffins are known as clowns of the sea worldwide, and as sea parrots in northern parts of Scotland.

'purr'

'purr'

- **IUCN status:** Vulnerable
- **UK status:** Red
- **Length:** 27 cm
- **Wingspan:** 55 cm
- **Visible:** March to August
- **Sexes:** Alike
- **Voice:** Low purrs with pig-like grunts.

PUFFIN
FRATERCULA ARCTICA

Europe is home to the largest population of a truly charismatic bird: the Atlantic puffin. Their brightly coloured beaks have earned them the name sea parrots in Scotland.

Puffins spend most of their lives at sea, coming to land only during their spring breeding season. This is the time that we are most likely to see them flocked together, sporting their striking orange beaks.

At around the age of four, puffins choose their mates for life. Their beaks become colourful during the breeding season and reflect UV light, acting as a beacon to other puffins, helping them attract a partner. A puffin pair will usually lay just a single egg in an underground burrow lined with soft feathers. Once hatched, the puffling's parents take it in turns to bring sand eels back to the nest.

Puffins fly low over the water, vigorously flapping their tiny wings up to 400 times per minute, reaching impressive speeds of 88 kilometres per hour. We can see this spectacle from land, or from a boat trip out to sea. Once a puffin spots a fish, it takes the plunge, diving to depths of up to 60 metres. Their tongues and serrated beaks hold the slippery fish in place. Puffins have been recorded holding up to eighty sand eels at once! Stocks of sand eel are currently on the decline, so some puffin populations are struggling for food.

Towards the end of August, the puffins, and their young, return to the sea. The adults shed their bright beak plates, leaving a smaller and less vibrant beak in its place, until the cycle starts again the following year.

GANNET
MORUS BASSANUS

These magnificent bright-white birds with impressive wingspans of nearly 2 metres – taller than the average adult woman – are the largest seabirds in the North Atlantic.

When hunting for fish in flocks, gannets circle up to 30 metres above the water before plummeting towards the ocean at speeds of up to 95 kilometres per hour. This is so rapid that, taken aback by the spectacle, you may lose track of which bird you are watching as they blast through the sky! They have several adaptations to protect them from the force of the impact with water. Air sacs in their faces and chests act in the same way as car airbags, and the nostrils inside their mouths close to prevent water coming in. These clever birds have learned to follow dolphins and whales, watching their every move as the sea creatures guide the birds to dinner.

Gannets migrate over winter, heading to the west of the Mediterranean or the Gulf of Guinea, before travelling back north to breed. They make their nests on islands and coasts. Two thirds of the world's nesting population of northern gannets are located in the UK from January to August: their largest colony is on Bass Rock in Scotland. There are also large colonies of gannets in Iceland, Germany, Norway and France.

Grab a pair of binoculars, or hop on board a tourist boat, to observe the splendid mating ritual of the northern gannet. Watch as the males shake their heads from side to side in an exaggerated motion. While waiting to pair up, fights can break out between males, sometimes ending in broken bones! Pairs can remain together for life, greeting one another each season by spreading their wings wide, bowing and knocking their bills together. A perfectly practiced duet.

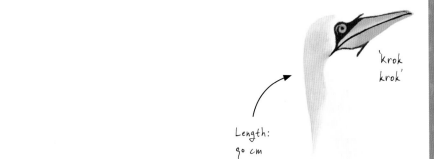

'krok krok'

Length: 90 cm

Wingspan: 175 cm

- **IUCN status:** Least Concern
- **UK status:** Amber
- **Visible:** January to August
- **Sexes:** Alike
- **Voice:** A throaty 'arrah-arrah', or a quieter 'krok krok'.

Length:
17 cm

Wingspan:
37 cm

'kree'

'kree'

In the USA, they are known as
red-backed sandpipers.

- **IUCN status:** Least Concern
- **UK status:** Amber
- **Visible:** All year
- **Sexes:** Alike
- **Voice:** High 'tissee' or 'treep' trills.
  Call is a high-pitched 'kree'.

DUNLIN
CALIDRIS ALPINA

Despite having a name that may mean 'dull brown thing' – awarded because of its grey-brown upperparts, pale head and breast in winter – the dunlin is in fact a complex and resilient character.

Across the tip of the dunlin's bill is a soft covering that contains nerve endings and blood vessels: the birds use this probe to locate prey. You may spot them on coastal mudflats, jabbing at sludge with their bills in a characteristic 'stitching' motion, moving up and down like the needle of a sewing machine to pick out marine worms.

This is the most common of the small coastal waders. As tidal feeders, they are busy after dark if the mud and ooze are exposed. They feed in enormous flocks – or 'flings' – of thousands over winter, then roost on nearby shorelines, fields and saltmarshes at high tide when their feeding grounds are submerged. The sheer number of birds gathered together makes it easy to distinguish dunlins from other small waders. They also develop distinctive black belly patches during the breeding season that no other similar-sized wader possesses.

Dunlins have a wide breeding range that includes moorland areas of north Europe. However, most of the dunlins we see in the European winter will have arrived from Scandinavia and Russia. Females arrive first as the males stay behind to care for the young. These are long-distance migrants who often return to the place of their hatching to nest. In Gaelic, their name may also refer to their breeding habitat of 'dun', meaning hill, and 'lin', meaning pool.

Some dunlins have learned to feed in seaside areas close to artificial lights. At night they use this extra illumination to help them see their prey.

CORMORANT
PHALACROCORAX CARBO

Cormorants capture fish deftly with their heavy, hook-tipped bills, diving down to depths of ten metres. They can hear better underwater than they can on land.

Modified barbs on their jet-black feathers allow air to escape from beneath, and enable water to penetrate their plumage, making them nifty swimmers. But once out of the water, they need to dry off quickly to avoid losing too much body heat. This is when we are most likely to see them, sitting on rocky outcrops or boats, with their wings outstretched, basking in sunlight.

These large birds have had an interesting relationship with humans. We have taken advantage of their remarkable fishing abilities since AD 960. From a simple bamboo raft, without a rod or bait, Chinese fishermen traditionally trained captive birds to dive into the water and secure their prey. They tied cords around the birds' throats to stop them from swallowing their catch. The fishermen would then swap the larger fish for a smaller reward. King James I of England adopted this technique, even employing a Master of Cormorants on the River Thames.

Europe is also home to a similar bird: the shag. These two can be mistaken for one another. Adult cormorants are shiny black, whereas shags have an emerald green sheen – they are known as green cormorants. Shags and cormorants mainly reside on the coast, but some cormorants have moved inland around lakes or gravel pits. At either location, sure signs of their presence are large, messy nests made of sticks located high up in the fork of a tree or on a cliff ledge.

These reptile-like birds belong to an ancient group that have been around since the dinosaurs. Their name comes from medieval French and means 'sea raven'.

'croak'

- **IUCN status:** Least Concern
- **UK status:** Green
- **Length:** 90 cm
- **Wingspan:** 145 cm
- **Visible:** All year
- **Sexes:** Alike
- **Voice:** Silent with guttural croak when on the nest.

The cormorant is also known as the sea crow in southwest England.

- **IUCN status:** Least Concern
- **UK status:** Amber
- **Length:** 32 cm
- **Wingspan:** 85 cm
- **Visible:** April to September
- **Sexes:** Alike
- **Voice:** Harsh, shrill calls, 'kee-yah' or 'kip'.

'kee-yah'

'kip'

In England they are also known as the sea swallow.

COMMON TERN
STERNA HIRUNDO

Keep your eyes to the skies over the summer months to spot these delightful 'sea swallows'. Once found primarily in coastal areas, many of these elegant birds now make their home inland, even breeding in towns. They are graceful in flight as they come in to land on gravel beaches and reservoirs throughout Europe. They travel here from their winter grounds in western or southern Africa to begin breeding in spring.

The common tern often shares its habitat with gull species but it can be distinguished by its deeply forked, swallow-like tail. It is sometimes confused with the Arctic tern, but it has a white belly, a shorter tail streamer and a longer bill, along with a striking black cap that it wears only during breeding season.

Fish are their main food, although they will occasionally consume shrimps, marine worms and leeches. To see a common tern make a catch, watch as it hovers low over the water, before briefly plunging in to a depth of only 50 centimetres below the surface. Be amazed as it emerges and swallows the prey whole – head first!

Common terns nest in colonies of up to 20,000 breeding pairs, which together create a noisy ruckus. You may hear them before you see them – and you may smell the droppings, or guano, before they are either heard or seen! As with many birds, they reuse the same nest site year on year. One pair was discovered returning for seventeen successive breeding seasons.

Courtship, which starts in April, is a spectacle. The male and female dance high in the sky, circling around one another before descending together, in zigzag glides, back towards their nest.

OYSTERCATCHER
HAEMATOPUS OSTRALEGUS

Oystercatchers fly like butterflies, with slow, deep wing beats, during their elaborate courtship displays. These displays occur from April to August, at which time pairs will make only a single attempt at breeding.

They have a long, bright-red bill and thin, pink legs that help them to stand out in the company of other waders. Their piping call is loud and, if predators approach their territory, it can reach an ear-splitting pitch.

They create simple nests, which are little more than scrapes in the ground. Some of the more opportunistic oystercatchers practice 'egg dumping', where they lay their eggs in the nest of another bird species – such as a gull – and leave them to be raised by different parents.

Over winter, oystercatchers migrate from northern Europe to the warmer south, bringing together birds from as far away as Norway and Iceland. They congregate in groups of several hundred individuals on shores, reefs, coastal mudflats and saltmarshes, making a loud 'kleep kleep' call.

Despite their name, these birds rarely eat oysters. Instead, their diet includes insect larvae, earthworms and, most often, mussels. They use their powerful bills to hammer at and pry open shells. Many oystercatchers spend the breeding season inland on the shores of lakes and reservoirs, or even on grassland, some distance from water. Some individuals have even opted to nest on the flat roofs of buildings in town. These locations keep the young safe from predators.

Oystercatchers have been known to live for forty years – much longer than most waders. Science has yet to learn the reason for this long life!

- **IUCN status:** Near Threatened
- **UK status:** Amber
- **Length:** 43 cm
- **Wingspan:** 83 cm
- **Visible:** All year
- **Sexes:** Alike
- **Voice:** Shrill 'kleep kleep' call.

'kleep'

'kleep'

The traditional English name for oystercatchers is the sea pie, or sea magpie.

'kyaoo kyaoo'

These birds are also known as the white maa on the Orkney Islands and the silver back in Ireland.

- **IUCN status:** Least Concern
- **UK status:** Red
- **Length:** 60 cm
- **Wingspan:** 140 cm

- **Visible:** All year
- **Sexes:** Alike
- **Voice:** Rich repertoire of calls; yelping 'kyaoo'.

HERRING GULL
LARUS ARGENTATUS

There is no such bird as a seagull. Many gulls have moved inland, so the word is no longer used by scientists. Instead, there are many species of gull. There are six resident in the UK alone and the herring gull is the most common. These birds are known as the 'voice of the seaside', with their raucous calls resonating across coastal towns, and inland, reaching playing fields and lakes.

The herring gull can be differentiated from other gulls by its large size and its bright-white feathers, which have dark patches on the wingtips with white spots known as 'mirrors'. They have a red spot on the lower half of their bill that sets them apart from similar species. Gull chicks peck at this spot on the bills of their parents to encourage them to regurgitate food.

Many herring gulls reside in urban environments, where they thrive year-round, in part on discarded human food. Although you are likely to see large flocks, these are not social birds, and contact between them is kept to a minimum. The exception to this is breeding time. You may see the female approach her chosen mate in his territory, making begging calls to begin courtship. If he responds to her, they will choose a nest site that they may return to for many years.

Although these birds have a wide range across Europe, populations within countries such as England, Finland and Sweden are decreasing, due to a decline in the local fish that they eat. Some scientists are calling for the gulls to be given an IUCN status of Near Threatened.

Hopefully the herring gulls' status as icons of the seaside will continue for generations – even though these aerial highwaymen do make a dive for our picnics!

GREAT SPOTTED WOODPECKER

DENDROCOPOS MAJOR

Walking through the forest in early spring you may hear a distant tapping: a great spotted woodpecker is nearby. These territorial birds live in the same location all year round. Unlike most birds, they do not sing to mark their territory. Instead, they drum. This noise has the dual function of warning off intruders and attracting a mate.

The woodpecker will choose a dead or hollow tree to make the loudest noise. The frenzied drumming happens at a rate of up to twenty trunk taps per second. Each bird deploys an individual rhythm, which is as distinctive as a human voice, identifying it to other woodpeckers. To shield themselves from the impact of the headbanging, their skulls are protected by several skeletal adaptations that absorb most of the force.

The woodpeckers also use their tree-chiselling technique to find food and excavate nest holes. Their favourite foods are insects and their larvae, which they extract using long, sticky tongues. In autumn and winter, when there are not as many bugs, they switch to a diet of nuts and berries. Leave some peanuts in a feeder and you may catch a glimpse of the great spotted woodpecker.

Males sport a bright-red patch on the back of their necks and young have a red cap. The head of the female is black. Look out for their bouncing flight from tree to tree. Once they land, they will cling to the tree and their stiff tail feathers will help prop them up against the trunk. An unusual toe arrangement, with two toes facing forwards and two facing backwards, makes them remarkable climbers.

In Staffordshire, this bird is traditionally known as a wood pie.

'kik' 'kik'

- **IUCN status:** Least Concern
- **UK status:** Green
- **Length:** 22 cm
- **Wingspan:** 37 cm

- **Visible:** All year
- **Sexes:** Differ, see opposite
- **Voice:** Short, sharp, explosive 'kik'.

In Somerset, a jay is also traditionally known as a devil scritch.

- **IUCN status:** Least Concern
- **UK status:** Green
- **Length:** 35 cm
- **Wingspan:** 55 cm

- **Visible:** All year
- **Sexes:** Alike
- **Voice:** Harsh jeering call.

JAY
GARRULUS GLANDARIUS

The jay is the most colourful member of the crow family. This bird boasts a striking array of bright feathers, from a dusky-pink body with electric-blue tipped wings, to a soft-grey crest and a black tail with a white rump.

You are likely to hear a jay before you see it, as these birds screech through the woodland with a harsh, jeering call. They are also known for their incredible mimicry abilities. They can imitate species from tawny owls to goshawks, so it can be almost impossible to identify them from sound alone without getting a glimpse.

Despite their noisy presence, they are rather shy birds, and rarely move far from the cover of treetops. Your best chance of spying a jay is in autumn, when they search for fallen acorns – their favourite food – on the ground. They hide these away in a cache for winter. A single jay can collect up to 5,000 acorns in a season and they don't always remember their hiding places, accidentally leaving acorns to grow into oak trees. It is thought that the jays' forgetfulness may have contributed to the spread of oak trees

after the last ice age! Jays have a darker side too: they sometimes steal and eat the eggs and nestlings of other birds.

At the start of spring, jays work with their lifelong mates to make nests, which they build in trees and shrubs using twigs, roots and even hair for lining. Male jays share the food they have stored over winter as part of the courtship ritual.

Jays enjoy one very curious activity. They land on ant nests and allow the ants to crawl all over them. No one knows the precise function of 'anting' but it is believed to help them reduce parasites on their feathers.

TAWNY OWL
STRIX ALUCO

The famous 'too-wit too-woo' owl call is in fact made up of a call between two tawny owls as they check one another's whereabouts in the woodland. They are well adapted to living here, with rich-brown feathers that camouflage them among the trees.

Pairs of tawny owls usually mate for life and stay within their established territory. Mating occurs in springtime and the female then lays her eggs in a cavity in a large tree. If you have a pair of binoculars, look high into the treetops during the day and you may see a group of small, fluffy owlets sitting in a huddle while their parents are roosting nearby. At the end of autumn, the grown owls fly the nest.

Tawny owls are well-crafted predators. From their woodland perches, they can turn their heads an impressive 270 degrees when on the lookout for small mammals to eat, such as voles and mice. Their hearing is finely attuned: the right ear is slightly lower on the head than the left, and is tilted downwards, which makes it highly sensitive to sounds on the forest floor below.

Once the tawny owl has honed in on its prey, it descends through the trees with the soft edge of its feathers ensuring a soundless flight. If you are out after dark walking through the trees, you may get a surprise as a tawny owl swoops ahead of you and snatches up a rodent from the forest floor.

As the wild world has changed, so have tawny owls, and they can now be seen in parks, on farmland and even in urban areas where there are enough large trees for roosting and nesting.

'hooo-hu'

'hooo-hu'

- **IUCN status:** Least Concern
- **UK status:** Amber
- **Length:** 37 cm
- **Wingspan:** 98 cm
- **Visible:** All year
- **Sexes:** Alike
- **Voice:** A clear, drawn out 'hooo-hu' ('too-wit too-woo').

Pheasants are also known
as gold rings in England.

- **IUCN status:** Least Concern
- **UK status:** Introduced
- **Length:** 80 cm
- **Wingspan:** 80 cm

- **Visible:** All year
- **Sexes:** Differ, see opposite
- **Voice:** Harsh, crowing call.

PHEASANT
PHASIANUS COLCHICUS

The recognisable male, or cock, pheasant is highly territorial and can fight for upwards of twenty minutes. They are so sensitive to the calls of potential rivals that they have been known to respond to the sound and vibrations created by distant artillery or advancing earthquakes!

The pheasant is historically native to Asia and parts of eastern Europe. They were introduced to Europe for game hunting and were prevalent in the UK by the 1400s. Pheasants are stunning birds. Males sport a rich, fiery, reddish-brown plumage intertwined with black markings that extend to the tips of their long tails. There is an iridescent blue-green sheen across their heads and a red patch around their eyes.

Cock pheasants are often accompanied by many hens, or females, known as a harem. In contrast to the male plumage, females have pale-brown feathers all over. Within the group, each hen raises her young alone. She makes a simple nest by scraping a hole in the ground, which she lines with grass and leaves. The most common nest spots are under hedges,

so those are the best places to scan for pheasant chicks.

Pheasants eat a wide range of foods. In winter, their diet is mainly seeds and grains, but in summer, it includes lots of invertebrates, too.

While they are capable of short-distance flights, pheasants prefer to run. As you drive along a track near woodland or farmland, you may see a flash of iridescent colour near a hedgerow or a copse of trees, just before a pheasant explodes out into the open countryside – or even on to the road ahead – with a barking call!

TREECREEPER

CERTHIA FAMILIARIS

The treecreeper is an active little bird that – as the name suggests – spends a lot of time in the forest, which is where you are most likely to spot it. Perfectly camouflaged against bark, each of the feathers on its back and wings is a warm brown, intricately patterned with black and white speckles. Its underside is bright white.

These birds don't migrate, but in autumn, they leave their breeding territories – straying no more than 20 kilometres away – to join flocks of other small birds, such as tits. The little birds huddle together to stay warm during the colder months. As you walk through the woods during winter and stumble across a group of small birds darting from tree to tree, listen for the shrill, penetrating call of a treecreeper among them.

The treecreepers' favourite foods are insects and spiders. You may see them using their vertical, mouse-like hops to travel up trees, spiralling around the trunk until they find a suitable crevice. The bird will then use its long, thin, downward-curved bill to probe the hole and snap up any insects hidden within. They then take off in an erratic, undulating flight. During winter, when invertebrates are scarce, treecreepers will feed on seeds – and will perhaps even visit your local bird feeder.

In April, the treecreeper once again returns to its home territory to find a mate. Once a breeding pair has found a suitable crevice behind loose bark, they make a nest out of spiders' web, moss and feathers. Chicks fledge after just fifteen days, but take a while to leave the nest for good. If you keep track of a family, you may see the fledgelings return to the nest for a while after first leaving, to receive a reliable meal from their parents each day.

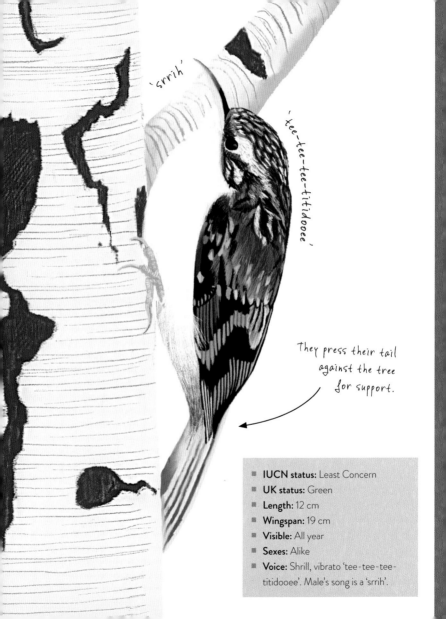

'srrih'

'tee-tee-tee-titidooee'

They press their tail
against the tree
for support.

- **IUCN status:** Least Concern
- **UK status:** Green
- **Length:** 12 cm
- **Wingspan:** 19 cm
- **Visible:** All year
- **Sexes:** Alike
- **Voice:** Shrill, vibrato 'tee-tee-tee-titidooee'. Male's song is a 'srrih'.

'pee-pee-pee pee-pee-pee' 'pee-pee-pee pee-pee-pee'

- **IUCN status:** Least Concern
- **UK status:** Green
- **Length:** 14 cm
- **Wingspan:** 25 cm

- **Visible:** All year
- **Sexes:** Alike
- **Voice:** Loud 'twit', 'chit' or 'dip' calls.
  Song has rising and falling 'pee-pee-pee'.

NUTHATCH
SITTA EUROPAEA

Nuthatches are agile little birds, scurrying along tree trunks with powerful claws. As one of the most adept climbers of the bird world, they are able to move upwards, downwards, sideways – and they spend so much of their time facing downwards that they're known as the 'upside-down bird'.

We are less likely to see them in the air, as they make only short flights from tree to tree. Old oak trees are a favourite haunt of theirs and should be your first port of call when trying to spot them. Look out for their striking colours. They are blue-grey on top, with orange sides, white cheeks and a distinctive black band across their eyes, as if they are wearing blindfolds. This bold appearance goes hand in hand with their character. These birds are unafraid, standing their ground when larger birds attempt to intimidate them away from their territories.

During autumn and winter, the birds forage for nuts, and hide extras in gaps in tree bark for later. The bird was named after its method of breaking into nutshells. It wedges its nut into a tree crevice, then chisels, or hacks, away at it with its beak until the shell gives way. Listen out for this tapping sound as you walk through the woods in the colder months. You can encourage the upside-down bird to your feeder by putting out nuts and seeds. At other times of the year, they feast on insects, such as caterpillars and beetles.

When choosing somewhere to nest, nuthatches opt for holes – often old woodpecker nest holes – in mature deciduous trees and line them with bark flakes. They also use nest boxes. To see the female create her nest from afar, through binoculars, watch her plaster mud around the entrance hole until it meets her exact requirements.

SKYLARK
ALAUDA ARVENSIS

On a midsummer morning, as you walk past fields towards a moor, you may hear a high-pitched chirruping without a bird in sight. Uninterrupted, complex and exuberant, the song will rise in intensity. High up above, you may spot a tiny, black dot hovering against the blue sky. This is the song-flight of the skylark.

After spying movement in the heather, a small, streaked-brown bird may then lift off almost vertically from the ground, and you'll hear another stream of song. This extraordinary aerial courtship display is performed by the male lark. To attract a mate and keep away rivals, these birds climb to 100 metres high. Their crescendo is an exhibition of fluttering and hovering, and they produce one of the most accomplished of all birdsongs before dropping to the ground to start all over again. This impressive display is visible all year round.

Larger than a sparrow but smaller than a starling, the skylark is a bird with fine features. It has a short crest and a broad tail, edged in white. The sexes are identical. The skylark is a ground nester and its numbers have fallen as farming practices have become more intense.

The lark has been truly celebrated in poetry and music, and in the 1800s, they were caged as songbirds. The song of the skylark was so prized that live birds were caught and transported to New Zealand, Australia and Canada so the settlers were able to hear the song of their homelands.

During that time, these birds were also eaten as a delicacy. But to truly 'taste' the joy of this bird, the best time to experience its rippling song is before sunrise on a spring morning.

'chirrup'

'chirrup'

'chirrup'

'chirrup'

In Shetland, this bird is known as a lady hen.

- **IUCN status:** Least Concern
- **UK status:** Red
- **Length:** 18 cm
- **Wingspan:** 33 cm
- **Visible:** All year

- **Sexes:** Alike
- **Voice:** Courtship song is melodious and incessant. Fast-paced rolling and chirruping.

- **IUCN status:** Least Concern
- **UK status:** Red
- **Length:** 18 cm
- **Wingspan:** 33 cm
- **Visible:** All year
- **Sexes:** Alike
- **Voice:** Courtship song is melodious and incessant. Fast-paced rolling and chirruping. Mnemonic for call is 'go-back... go-back'.

'Go-back, go-back, go-back...

... go-back, go-back, go-back'

RED GROUSE
LAGOPUS LAGOPUS

Hike out across heather moorland on a late summer afternoon, and if you're lucky, you may flush out a heathland specialist: the red grouse. These birds rocket out of the heather in a flurry of whirring wingbeats.

The plump, hen-sized grouse is resilient. Its legs and feet are covered in dense feathers that protect it in deep snow. They are closely related to the European willow grouse but the plumage of the red grouse does not turn white in winter.

These icons of wilderness survive almost entirely by eating heather – the shoots, seeds and flowers. They spend most of their lives camouflaged, feeding quietly. Males have bright red eyebrows and reddish-brown plumage, while females are mottled brown with less visible brows. The male grouse's red-flash eyebrow is a signal to mates and rivals. In spring, these feisty birds can become aggressive towards almost any red intruder. Angry males will even display to walkers with red socks!

Grouse are ground nesters. When a predator approaches, adult grouse can launch into a broken-wing display. They pretend to be injured, squawking and flapping as if they are unable to fly. The predator spots an easy meal and follows the 'injured' bird as it moves away from the nest. The chicks escape, and the adult then 'recovers' and flies away.

Numbers of this evocative species are falling across Europe as their upland habitat is threatened. In Britain, they can be caught in the crossfire of the commercial game shooting industry. These fierce survivors of the harshest winters have only a fragile grasp on the future. Each glimpse of them reminds us how full of surprise our moorlands can be.

GOLDEN EAGLE
AQUILA CHRYSAETOS

As the snaking purple heather leads your gaze up the mountain, beyond the green, into the scree and onwards to the jagged outcrop, you may see wings open out and an immense golden-brown bird take to the air. It will then drop, catch an air current, and lift slowly above the glen with powerful wingbeats. Turning on the thermal almost effortlessly, it will rise up into the blue. This is the magnificent golden eagle.

Flying alone or in pairs, golden eagles soar over mountains as they hunt for their prey of rabbit, hare or grouse. They ride the air currents like paper airplanes, using almost no energy. There is a golden sheen to their plumage around the head and neck, and their long wingtip feathers splay like fingers. But their precise plumage details change with their sex, their age and with the season.

Golden eagles mainly breed in mountains and upland forests. The birds establish a home range containing several nest sites, or 'eyries'. These sites can be used for decades by the same or successive eagles. The average cliff nest for an eagle is 1 to 1.5 metres wide, while a tree nest is 2 to 3 metres across. Eagles pair for life and are attentive parents. The female broods and feeds her young in the stick-and-branch nest while the male hunts for prey. Once the chicks are older, both parents continue to provide for the vast appetites of the growing birds. Their average lifespan is between fifteen and twenty years.

In Celtic folklore, eagles are symbols of strength, ancient wisdom and endurance, and are said to guard the high country. But these days, they are threatened by illegal killing, so it is they that need our protection. These elusive birds bring a precious splendour to our uplands and are to be treasured.

In the UK, these majestic birds are also known as mountain eagles.

- **IUCN status:** Least Concern
- **UK status:** Green
- **Length:** 90 cm
- **Wingspan:** 2.3 m

- **Visible:** All year
- **Sexes:** Alike
- **Voice:** Occasional short, high-pitched whistles.

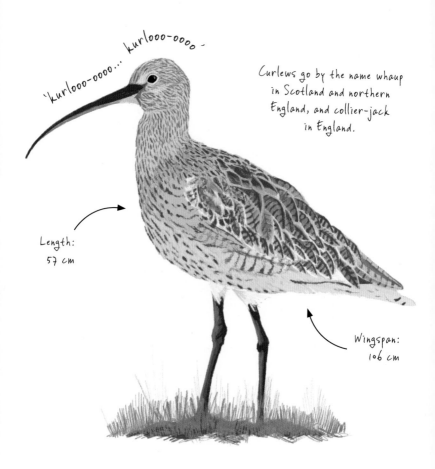

'kurlooo-oooo... kurlooo-oooo -

Curlews go by the name whaup in Scotland and northern England, and collier-jack in England.

Length: 57 cm

Wingspan: 106 cm

- **IUCN status:** Near Threatened
- **UK status:** Red
- **Visible:** All year
- **Sexes:** Differ, see opposite

- **Voice:** Rising, melancholy whistle that descends into a rippling trill. Listen for the mnemonic 'Kurlooo-oooo'.

CURLEW
NUMENIUS ARQUATA

During an early spring walk in the hills, as April showers give way to sunshine, you may find yourself listening to a soft, two-note, melancholic trill. This call sounds ghostly and out of place on a bright afternoon. It is likely to be the haunting voice of the curlew: yet there is no bird in sight.

In open country, this mournful wail carries across long distances, so it can be almost impossible to pinpoint the geographic location of the bird from its song. But when curlews do show themselves, they are unmistakable. They are one of Europe's largest wading birds at around 60 centimetres tall.

On long, delicate legs they pace about the landscape, probing the undergrowth or mud with their beaks. Most bird beaks lack any kind of nerve endings – similar to the human fingernail. But the curlew's long, scimitar-like beak has a flexible, sensitive tip that senses the vibrations made by the smallest movements of their prey. It is the crescent shape of the beak that gave the bird its scientific name, *Numenius*, which means 'of the new moon'.

Though the sexes have similar plumage, curlews are one of the few bird species in which females are larger than males. Males also have shorter beaks than females. They are ground nesters and their eggs are well camouflaged, even at close range. Young curlews can walk immediately after hatching and will scatter whenever danger threatens.

Curlews roam with the seasons. During the spring and summer, they haunt hill country, but autumn and winter lure them to the less hostile estuaries and salt marshes. In the mists of those wetlands, their spectral voices bewitch the darkest seasons until the longer days return.

RAVEN
CORVUS CORAX

During a gusty winter storm, you may hear a deep 'cronk' from overhead as a huge, black bird circles above. On the other side of the wood comes an answering 'cronk', and the raven pair surfs on the wind, rising and falling, buffeted by the gale.

Ravens have a distinctive diamond-shaped tail that allows for easy identification while they are in flight. At a distance, their plumage looks a sombre black, but seen close up, they have a rich, purple sheen to their glossy feathers.

In folklore, ravens are often depicted as omens of doom; a flock of them is known as an unkindness of ravens. Their brooding appearance and melancholic croak have encouraged an association with death or bad luck. However, the birds themselves are inquisitive, highly intelligent and very playful. They have been filmed sliding on their backs in snow and are known to break off small twigs from bushes for games of mid-air throw and catch. When predators get too close to their nests, clever ravens will drop small stones on the heads of the approaching enemies.

Ravens are opportunists. They will eat seeds, berries, insects, eggs and carrion. They are also capable hunters, taking small mammals and birds whenever the chance arises. The raven's massive beak acts as a cross between a hammer and an axe, while at other times it is a delicate instrument used to pick up tiny seeds.

Ravens pair for life. Their courtship display is one of the aerial glories of early spring. They tumble and twist, rolling and spiralling down from the sky. It is difficult to watch this performance without seeing the ravens as thrill seekers!

- **IUCN status:** Least Concern
- **UK status:** Green
- **Length:** 65 cm
- **Wingspan:** 130 cm
- **Visible:** All year
- **Sexes:** Alike
- **Voice:** Deep, resonant 'cronk'.

'cronk'

These birds go by several other names, including corbie in Scotland and croupie craw in northern England.

They are also called ringtails in the UK.

'chak, chak, chak'

- **IUCN status:** Least Concern
- **UK status:** Red
- **Length:** 50 cm
- **Wingspan:** 110 cm
- **Visible:** Northern Europe in spring and summer; southern Europe in autumn and winter. Some are resident all year in the UK.
- **Sexes:** Differ, see opposite
- **Voice:** The male makes a rapid 'chak, chak, chak', while the female makes a whistling 'pee-eh' when food is passed bewteen them.

HEN HARRIER
CIRCUS CYANEUS

A blue-grey bird climbs and swoops across the moor with prey in his talons. With a twist, he's joined by a would-be mate. They move together, graceful aeronauts mirroring each other's switchbacks. Then, their talons meet, and the female takes the prey. With their food-pass complete, the pair drops to the ground. These are hen harriers, and this is their sky dance.

In flight, the long, swept-back wings of the harriers look almost too big for their slender bodies. The male's display flight, full of spins and somersaults, demonstrates his good health and he uses this to attract a mate. His smoky-grey plumage differs from that of the female. She has mottled-brown feathers, a white rump, a banded tail and is larger. The young share her colouration.

These birds are ground nesters, and the female's plumage camouflages her as she sits on eggs. The male, meanwhile, provides her with voles and other small mammals. Hunting by 'quartering' the moorland, he keeps low, using his hearing as much as his eyesight. He'll drop to grab prey hiding in the vegetation. When he flies back to the nest with a meal, he calls to the female, who flies towards him to take the prey mid-air. The choreography of the food-pass is breathtaking.

Hen harriers are persecuted in Britain and their numbers are declining throughout Europe. Although they have been awarded full legal protection, the birds come into conflict with landowners where grouse shooting is popular. Hen harriers are now endangered in the UK, and conservation projects are in progress to reverse this.

Rare, iconic and spectacular in their wheeling dance, harriers embody the wild spirit of the moors.

INDEX

NEXT STEPS...

TO TAKE YOUR ID SKILLS FURTHER:

- *RSPB What's that Bird? The Simplest ID Guide Ever,* Rob Hume (DK, 2012).

- *RSPB Pocket Birds of Britain and Europe* (DK, 2017)

EUROPEAN BIRDS:

- *Collins Bird Guide*, Lars Svensson, Killian Mullarney, Dan Zetterström and Peter J Grant (Collins, 2015). Also available as an app.

BIRDS AND CULTURE:

- *Birds and People,* Mark Cocker and David Tipling (Jonathan Cape, 2013)

- *Tweet of the Day: A Year of Britain's Birds*, Brett Westwood and Stephen Moss (John Murray, 2016)

ATTRACT BIRDS TO YOUR GARDEN:

- *How to Attract Birds to Your Garden: Foods they like, plants they love, shelter they need*, Dan Rouse (DK, 2020)

HOW TO PROTECT BIRDS:

- *Back to Nature: How to Love Life – and Save It!* Chris Packham and Megan McCubbin (Two Roads, 2020) The authors founded the The Self-Isolating Bird Club (SIBC). SIBC on Facebook and @SIBirdClub on Twitter.

GOING DIGITAL:

- *Warblr:* record a song and Warblr will reveal the species you've captured. www.warblr.co.uk

- *Chirp! Bird Songs UK & Europe* www.spinysoftware.com

- *Sunbird Images* offers premium ID apps: www.sunbird.tv

- For a list of top apps: www.fatbirder.com

ONLINE RESOURCES:

- Royal Society for the Protection of Birds (RSPB). Site includes an excellent bird identifier. www.rspb.org.uk

- British Trust for Ornithology (BTO). Champions of conservation and science. www.bto.org

- BirdLife International. www.birdlife.org

- The Wildlife Trusts. Where to see birds and wildlife in the UK. www.wildlifetrusts.org

- Wildfowl and Wetlands Trust (WWT). WWT conserve, restore and create wetlands. www.wwt.org.uk

WEBCAMS:

Spot birds all around the world:

- Ospreys, puffins, peregrines, terns, owls and waterfowl: www.wildlifetrusts.org/webcams

- Cornell University and their partners. Hummingbirds, eagles, albatrosses and more from European, US and Australasian webcams: www.allaboutbirds.org/cams

CITIZEN SCIENCE:

- The RSPB's annual Big Garden Birdwatch: www.rspb.org.uk/get-involved/activities/birdwatch/

- BTO's Garden BirdWatch survey: www.bto.org/how-you-can-help/take-part-project